DISCARD

D1032768

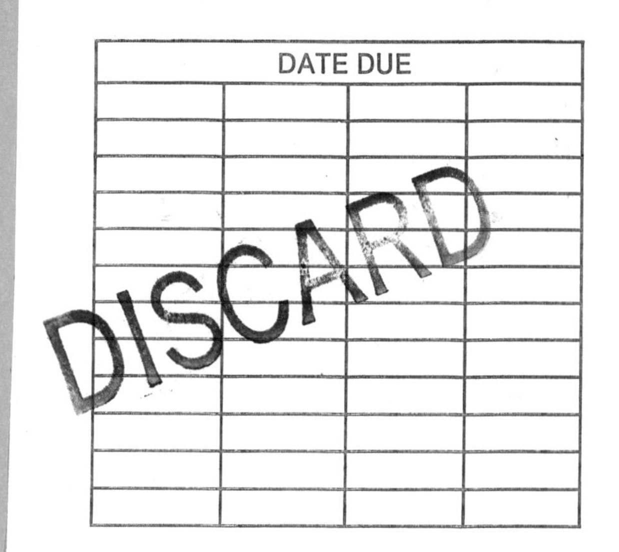
DATE DUE
DISCARD

TRADITIONAL TALES *from* THE CARIBBEAN

Vic Parker

Illustrated by
Christopher Corr

Thameside Press

Distributed in the United States by
Smart Apple Media
1980 Lookout Drive
North Mankato, MN 56003

Editor: Stephanie Turnbull
Designer: Zoë Quayle
Educational consultant: Margaret Bellwood

Library of Congress Cataloging-in-Publication Data

Parker, Vic.
The Caribbean / written by Vic Parker.
p. cm. -- (Traditional tales from around the world)
Includes index.
Summary: A collection of tales from the Caribbean, including
Creation myths, Anansi stories, and animal fables.
ISBN 1-930643-36-5
1. Tales--Caribbean Area. [1. Folklore--Caribbean Area.] I. Title.

PZ8.1.P2234 Car 2001
398.2'09729--dc21

2001027180

Printed in Hong Kong

9 8 7 6 5 4 3 2 1

CONTENTS

CARIBBEAN STORIES

The stories in this book are from the Caribbean—a curve of tropical islands between North and South America. Here fishermen sail their boats from white, sandy beaches. Farmers grow plantations of banana trees and sugar cane. Monkeys and parrots chatter to each other in steamy rainforest jungles.

The people who live in these islands came from all over the world. The first settlers were the Arawak and Carib peoples, who lived there for centuries. In 1492 the explorer Christopher Columbus arrived and soon after Spanish, English, French, and Dutch people settled there. They made the native people slaves and put them to work on farms. They brought men and women from West Africa to be slaves too. It was not until the nineteenth century that slavery was banned and Caribbean people became free again.

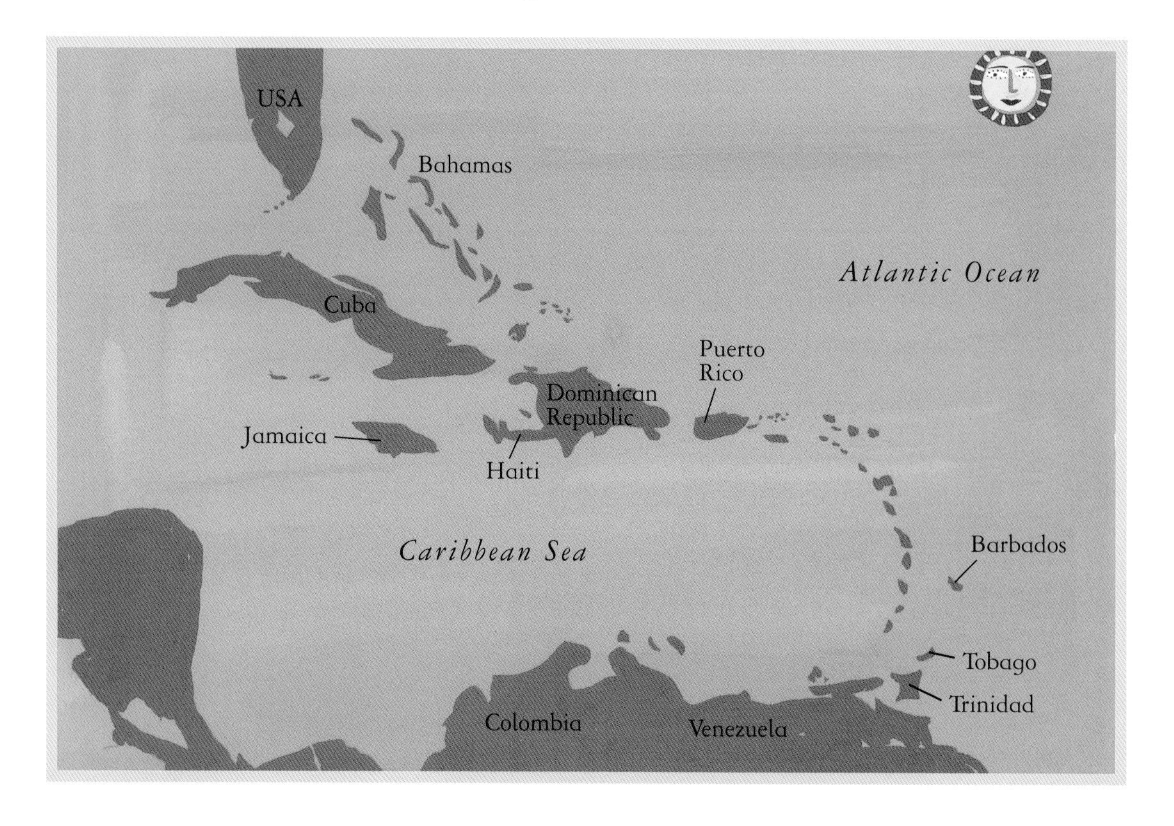

Caribbean people have always loved telling stories. Some people told tales of the animals and birds they found on the islands. Others spread stories of vampires and ghosts and spirits. The West Africans brought tales of a trickster called Anansi.

Storytellers have only recently written down these traditional tales. For hundreds of years, the stories lived in the memories of grandparents, aunts and uncles, mothers and fathers, and teachers. When each person told a story, they used their own style and added bits or left out bits as they wished. So the stories have changed over the years, and today there are many different versions of the same tale. In this book you can read new versions of some of the best-loved Caribbean stories.

The Tortoise Who Wanted to Fly

On a certain Caribbean island, at the end of the day, the sun dips into the sea and paints the sky pink and gold. The children come running to Grandpa's house by the beach. Big and small, the boys and girls dash onto Grandpa's front porch, begging, "Tell us a story! Please, Grandpa! Tell us a story!" And Grandpa whispers, "Shhh! Shhh!" like the waves of the ocean.

The children sit around Grandpa's rocking chair as he lights his pipe with his wrinkly brown hands. Puff . . . puff . . . he sends clouds of smoke gently rising into the darkening air. Then Grandpa's twinkly eyes shut, and creak . . . creak . . . goes his rocking chair, back and forth.

Grandpa is thinking of when he himself was just a little boy. Each night, he ran barefoot with his friends along the sand, all the way to Aunt Rosie's house. How well he remembers the stories Aunt Rosie told them under the stars! Grandpa smiles to himself and the children wait patiently. The cool evening breeze rustles the long leaves of the banana trees, and hundreds of hidden insects begin to buzz.

At last Grandpa opens his eyes and says,
"Crick crack!"
"Break my back!" answer the excited girls and boys.
And Grandpa begins his story....

Long, long ago, at the very beginning of the world, animals weren't at all the way they are now. Can you believe that Cat and Dog were once friends? Or that Owl used to fly during the day and sleep at night? Or that Donkey once had a beautiful singing voice?

Tortoise was very different too. Today his shell is bumpy and marked, but once it was as smooth as a shiny pebble. In fact it was so glossy that the birds liked to use it as a mirror. Pigeon, Woodpecker, Pelican, Owl, and many other birds were regular visitors to Tortoise's house. Tortoise let the birds polish his back with their soft wings. When his shell gleamed like glass, Tortoise stood very still while the beady-eyed birds checked their reflections. Carefully, they preened each feather into place. How the birds admired Tortoise's useful back!

In turn, how Tortoise admired the birds! He would gladly have swapped his shiny shell for their feathers.

For Tortoise longed to fly more than anything else in the world. The birds often told him what it was like to soar above the earth. They sang him songs about hovering in the sunlight and being lifted up high by the wind. Every day, Tortoise sighed a deep sigh and looked up wistfully at the sky. Every night, he dreamed he was gliding through the air, free as a bird.

One morning, Eagle swooped down to see Tortoise.

"I am having a party for all the birds," Eagle cried. "I want you to come too, as a special thank-you for being our mirror."

"Why, how very kind of you, Eagle," Tortoise said, with a broad grin.

"I'll see you on Saturday, then," Eagle replied, "at two o'clock at my house on top of the mountain."

He soared into the air and sped away with a few powerful flaps of his strong wings.

Suddenly Tortoise's face fell.

"How will I get there?" he called after Eagle. "It's too far for me to climb—and I can't fly!"

But Eagle was too high up to hear him.

"It's no good," sighed Tortoise miserably. "I won't be able to go to the party after all." Huge tears began to well up in his eyes.

Just then Flamingo flapped past. As soon as she heard why Tortoise looked so sad, she was determined to help.

"Perhaps there is a way you *can* fly, Tortoise," she said. "You have been so good to the birds that I'm sure everyone won't mind giving you one or two feathers each. If you stick them on, you'll be just like us!"

Tortoise looked up hopefully.

"Do you really think it would work?" he murmured.

"Of course," Flamingo squawked. "I'll go and ask all the other birds right now." She hurried away in a whirl of pink feathers.

Before long the birds had given Tortoise a pile of feathers higher than himself. There were short ones and long ones, thin ones and fat ones, plain ones and striped ones, smooth ones and fluffy ones. There were feathers of brown, red, green, white, black, blue, and gold. Flamingo and Peacock and Crow hurried to stick them all over Tortoise with lots of extra-sticky glue.

When the friends had finally finished, Tortoise looked like a very ugly bird indeed! But he didn't mind. He couldn't wait to get up in the air and try out his new flying skills! He scrambled to the top of a nearby cliff as fast as his stubby legs would take him.

"Don't forget to open out your arms!" Peacock called after him.

"And flap like crazy!" Crow added helpfully.

"Good luck!" shouted Flamingo.

Tortoise felt his heart begin to thump. He didn't dare look down in case the height made him feel dizzy. He just shut his eyes and jumped.

Down, down, down went Tortoise like a stone.

"Aaaaaaaargh!" he cried, plummeting toward the earth. As the wind rushed past him, feathers began to fly off in all directions. Then—SMASH! Tortoise hit the ground and his shell shattered into pieces.

Slowly, he sat up and rubbed his head. His soft, little body felt naked and cold.

"I don't think I like flying after all," he groaned. "I'll just keep my feet on the ground in the future."

Flamingo, Peacock, and Crow rushed to help Tortoise. They gathered all the broken pieces of his shell and stuck it together again. From that day to this, you can still see the cracks. And Tortoise always walks around very slowly and carefully, trying to avoid another accident.

A little boy grabs hold of Grandpa's hand.

"Didn't Tortoise go to Eagle's party after all?" he asks, anxiously.

"Of course he went to the party!" Grandpa laughs. "Eagle held it at Tortoise's house instead. All the birds came, and Tortoise was the guest of honor."

Grandpa puts down his pipe and begins to walk slowly into his house.

"Wire bend," he calls out.

"Story end," the children sigh. Time to run home....

The Land Beneath the Clouds

Next evening, when the boys and girls arrive at Grandpa's house, they find Grandpa carving a piece of wood with his pocketknife. Grandpa scrapes and chips away and says, "Crick crack!"

"Break my back!" reply the children at once.

And so Grandpa's story begins....

Long, long ago, in a far-off country, there lived a race of people just like you and me. They had brown, glossy skins and thick, black hair and they loved listening to stories, just like you. However, their homeland was very different from this lush island of ours. In their country, the rain had stopped falling. All day long the sun blazed down, turning the ground dry and cracked and dusty. The crops struggled to grow. The fruit trees withered. The forests turned brown and the animals disappeared. The rivers dried up and the fish died. Eventually, the birds were nearly all gone, too. The desperate people had to search further and further each day for things to eat.

One morning, a young hunter was stalking through new territory when he suddenly stopped in his tracks. He had nearly fallen into a big hole! Yet the hole wasn't dark and muddy at the bottom. It was white and swirling —just like the clouds!

The hunter lay on his stomach and crawled forward to peer over the edge. As the clouds moved, the hunter's eyes opened wide with surprise. Way down below, there was a deep, green sea. No, it wasn't a sea—it was the waving leaves of treetops! The hunter couldn't believe his eyes. Far underneath the leaves, he could just glimpse tiny animals and the sparkling blue of a stream! The hunter jumped to his feet in shock and ran home like the wind.

When the thrilled hunter told the chief and elders about the lovely, green land he had found, there was an uproar in the village.

"He's gone mad with hunger!" some people scoffed.

"But what if it's true?" others protested. "We could leave this dying place behind."

"There might be all sorts of dangers down there!" cried others, fearfully.

The people sat and argued about what to do until long after the moon had sailed into the sky. Finally, the chief stood up and raised his hand for silence.

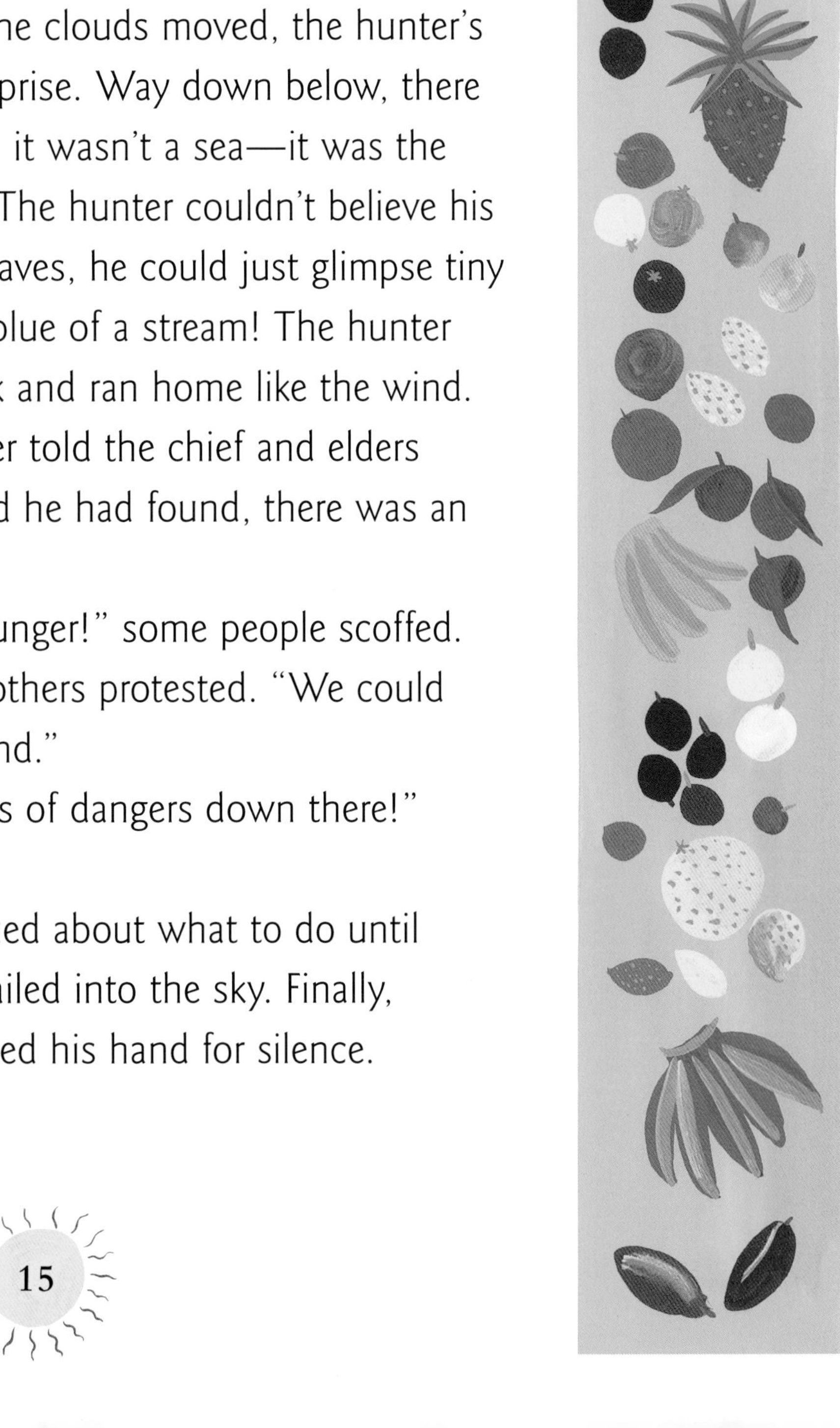

"Tomorrow we will go and see for ourselves," the chief announced. "If the land exists, we will find a way to go and explore, for if we stay here we will surely die."

Early next morning, the young hunter eagerly strode out with the chief. Every man, woman, and child followed nervously behind. They carried heavy bundles of belongings, and many of them were grumbling.

The villagers walked for hours through the blazing sun until at last they were near the spot.

"Over there!" the hunter cried excitedly. "Go and look!"

At once, the weary people dropped everything and raced over to the strange hole. They crowded around, pushing and jostling, crying out in disbelief at the wonderful world below the swirling clouds. Then they burst into tears of joy and danced with delight.

Next, the hard work began. The men and children rushed away in all directions to find vines and creepers. The women wound and braided them together until their hands were sore. Eventually they had a long, long rope. Everyone watched in silence as the chief solemnly laid the hundreds of coils on the ground by the hole. He tied one end tightly to a huge rock and let the other end go tumbling down through the clouds.

The coils immediately began to slither away. Faster and faster they slipped through the hole. The people watched the rope anxiously, hoping that it would be long enough. Finally all the rope had unraveled. Who would be the first person to venture into the unknown?

The young hunter stepped forward and slung his bow and arrows onto his back.

"I'll go first," he said bravely. He grasped the rope firmly and slid down through the clouds. The people waited and waited and finally heard a faint call:

"Come down! It's safe!"

One by one every man, woman, and child climbed down the long, long rope. As they emerged from the clouds, a fantastic scene met their eyes.

The new world was more beautiful than anyone had imagined. Oranges, bananas, and mangoes dangled from the trees. Deer nibbled at luscious green bushes. Cattle wandered through tall sugar cane. Insects hummed around perfumed flowers. Rainbow-colored birds darted overhead, chirping merrily. Fish leaped in clear streams.

"We will stay here until the rains come back to our own land," the chief said, sighing with happiness.

The people whooped with joy and ran away to explore the wonderful land.

Everyone fell in love with their new home—everyone, that is, except one woman. She had always been miserable and never wanted to join in with the others. All she could do was complain. The flowers were too bright. The rain was too wet. The animals frightened her and there were strange noises at night. Her friends got so fed up that they stopped talking to her, but the woman didn't care.

"I don't need you!" she muttered to herself. "I shall go back home and live happily on my own."

One night, she returned to the spot where the rope still dangled from the sky. Up she went, huffing and puffing, right to the hole in the clouds.

Strange, she thought, as she stuck her head and one arm through. *I don't remember the hole being this small!* She wriggled her other arm through and then her shoulders. She pushed and heaved—but no matter how hard she tried, she couldn't budge. The reason for this, of course, was that the woman had grown fat from all the wonderful things she had eaten on earth. She was jammed tight in the hole. She couldn't go up and she couldn't go down.

When the others discovered the woman's legs and big bottom wedged into the sky, they realized that they would never be able to go home again.

Everyone was secretly relieved. They didn't want to go back anyway! And that is how humans came to join the animals living on the islands of the Caribbean.

Grandpa holds up his carving so the girls and boys can see it. The wood now has a body, two arms and legs and a head with a smiling face. It looks just like you and me. Grandpa gives the doll to the little girl in front of him.

"Wire bend," he says.

"Story end," the little girl replies, jumping to her feet. She runs away, waving the doll high in the air, and the other children skip after her....

ANANSI THE SPIDER-MAN

Grandpa says, "Tonight, I am not going to say 'Crick crack!' because I am going to tell you an Anansi story."

"What's an Anansi story?" one of the children asks.

Grandpa looks up at a dusty cobweb in a corner of his porch roof and chuckles to himself.

"Listen carefully and I will tell you," he says.

And so he begins his tale....

Mr. Anansi lived a long, long time ago. He was a spider who knew how to turn himself into a man, but in those days, no one thought that was very strange. This was because animals and birds and humans used to be much more alike then than they are now. Everyone lived together and worked together and played together, and everyone spoke the same language.

Tiger was the strongest creature, so he ruled over everyone as king. If Tiger swung his tail, Parrot stopped chattering. If Tiger bared his teeth, Crocodile slunk into the river. If Tiger snarled, the mountains rumbled in reply.

Lots of things were named after King Tiger. There were beautiful flowers called Tiger Lilies, bright stones called Tiger's Eyes, and dusky insects called Tiger Moths. The stories that the animals told each other every evening were called Tiger stories.

Anansi, on the other hand, was the weakest creature. No one looked up to Anansi, and nothing was named after him. Anansi got fed up with this.

One night, when storytime was over, Anansi scuttled right up to Tiger. He bowed, but Tiger pretended not to notice him.

"O great Tiger...." Anansi began, but Tiger just licked his lips. "O great and wise Tiger...." Tiger simply inspected his deadly sharp claws. "O great, wise and brave Tiger...." Tiger slowly turned his huge head, and his golden eyes burned into Anansi like fire. The wiry spider-man took a step back and all the other animals snickered. "O great, wise, brave . . . and handsome Tiger," Anansi continued, "perhaps you would be kind enough to do me a favor?"

The edges of Tiger's mouth curled into a hint of a smile. He looked up and said to everyone, "Did you just hear that squeaking? It was almost as if some cheeky little creature was daring to talk to me!"

The other animals whooped with laughter.

“I know I am only a small, weak spider-man,” Anansi shouted up at Tiger, “but even so, I would like something named after me.”

Tiger gave a roar of delight at Anansi’s boldness.

“Tell me, Anansi,” he said, “what would you like to bear your name?”

“The stories,” Anansi yelled. “I want the stories to be named after me.”

“Hmm,” growled Tiger. He wasn’t happy about that at all. Out of everything that was named after him, he loved the stories the most. Tiger half-closed his eyes and thought. He didn’t want to look like a nasty, mean king and say no. Then again, he didn’t want to give Anansi the stories either. At last, Tiger had a wonderful idea.

“Anansi,” he announced, “you know Mr. Snake who lives down by the river?” Anansi gulped. Mr. Snake was famous for having a huge appetite and for always being in a bad mood. “I have always wanted to have a chat with Mr. Snake,” Tiger continued. “If you bring me Mr. Snake, you can have the stories.”

“I will do as you ask, O King,” agreed Anansi bravely, and he dashed off as fast as his thin legs could carry him.

The other animals laughed until their sides hurt.

"There's no way that feeble Anansi can possibly catch enormous, angry Mr. Snake," they hooted. "How clever Tiger is!"

At the river, Anansi sat down next to Snake's hole. All night long he waited in the moonlight. By sunrise, when Snake popped his head out, the spider-man had thought up a plan.

"Good morning, Mr. Snake," said Anansi.

"Get out of my way, Anansi," replied Snake dangerously. "I'm hungry." He began to slither out of his hole to go looking for his breakfast.

"My, what a long body you have, Mr. Snake!" said Anansi. "I told them that you were the longest creature of all, but they didn't believe me."

"What are you talking about?" said Snake, crossly. "Who are *they*?"

"King Tiger and his friends," lied Anansi.

"But of course I'm the longest creature!" sneered Snake.

"Well, *I* know that," said Anansi, "but *they* don't think so. *They* said that you weren't even as long as that bamboo."

Anansi pointed to the plant that grew nearby.

"You don't say!" spat Snake. He stretched out his coils into a straight line. "See?" he hissed.

Anansi stood back and stared first at Snake, then at the bamboo, then at Snake again.

"Well, I'm sure you're right, Mr. Snake," Anansi sighed, "but it's really hard to tell, because you're over here and the bamboo is over there."

"Then go and get it, stupid!" spat Snake impatiently.

Anansi hurried to cut down the bamboo. He laid the bare pole on the ground.

"Tut, tut!" he said, scratching his head. "I think the bamboo might be longer after all."

"Ridiculous!" Snake sneered. "Measure me up against it!" He started to stretch out next to the pole.

Anansi shook his head.

"It's no use, Mr. Snake. Both you and the bamboo are so long that I can't see both ends at once! When I run up to see where your head is, you might wriggle up the pole. And when I run down to see where your tail is, you might slip down the pole. Tiger and his friends will think you're a cheat."

"Suffering sidewinders!" Snake hissed in a fury. "You'll have to tie me onto the pole, and then you can see for sure!"

Anansi's heart thumped fast inside his chest as he tied Snake's long, thin body tightly to the bamboo.

Snake stretched and strained and struggled. His head reached just past the end of the pole.

"Well done!" cried Anansi. "You're definitely longer!" He lashed Snake's neck to the bamboo. "And you're also caught fast!" he added triumphantly.

Anansi heaved the pole over his shoulder and set off happily through the forest.

Tiger was so furious when he saw the spider-man bringing him Mr. Snake that none of the other animals dared talk to him for a week. But he couldn't go back on his word, so from that day to this, Tiger's tales have been called Anansi stories.

THE LAST LAUGH

"Tell us another story about Anansi and Tiger," the children beg Grandpa.

Grandpa thinks hard and says, "Did I tell you that in the old days, Tiger wore stylish clothes and walked proudly on two legs?"

"No!" gasp the surprised boys and girls.

And so Grandpa begins his story....

When Tiger put on his best suit and went strutting on two legs down the street, all the animals would whistle in admiration. Once a week, Tiger used to call on the beautiful Miss Selina. Tiger and Miss Selina were very good friends, and Tiger thought they made a fine-looking pair—Miss Selina with her dark hair and eyes and he with his grand stripes and important walk. Tiger wanted Miss Selina to marry him one day.

Anansi the spider-man was also fond of Miss Selina, but he was worried that Miss Selina liked Tiger best. He decided to do something before it was too late.

Anansi visited Miss Selina and remarked, "Isn't Tiger a splendid creature? You'd never guess he was once my daddy's old riding horse!"

"What?" Miss Selina cried in shock. "You mean that handsome Tiger went on all fours in the dust, carrying people on his back? I can't believe it!"

"It's true," nodded Anansi innocently. "I'll prove it to you, if you like." Humming a little tune, he went back to his house, climbed into bed, and waited.

Later on, Anansi heard a mighty roar of rage in the distance. The ground shook as enormous paws thundered closer and closer, then—SMASH! A striped foot burst right through Anansi's front door.

"Anansi!" Tiger bellowed. "Miss Selina has just told me to go away!" BASH! Tiger destroyed more of Anansi's door. "Because of you, she doesn't want to see me anymore!" CRASH! Tiger kicked the door right in. "GOT YOU!" he roared. "Come and tell Miss Selina you lied!"

Anansi pretended to be in pain. He clutched his stomach and howled, "Oh Tiger, I have an awful fever and I believe I am dying!"

"Dying?" gasped Tiger. "You can't die! You have to come and tell Miss Selina that I was never your daddy's old riding horse!"

Anansi made his teeth chatter and he started to shiver.

"Don't die, Anansi!" begged Tiger desperately. "At least, not before I've gotten you to Miss Selina's house!"

He slung Anansi onto his back.

"Tiger, I am weak," Anansi groaned. "I might fall off."

The anxious Tiger slung some rope around his neck for Anansi to hold on to.

"Tiger, a wasp might sting me, and that would be the end of me," Anansi moaned.

The frantic Tiger gave Anansi a stick to swat insects.

"Tiger, my bones are growing cold!" Anansi wailed. "You'd better be quick!"

In a panic, Tiger dropped down onto four legs. He knew he could run faster that way. He sprang away with Anansi bobbing about on his back.

When they drew near to Miss Selina's house, Anansi yanked on the rope around Tiger's neck. Tiger roared with pain, and Miss Selina came running outside. She could hardly believe her eyes. There was Anansi riding Tiger right past her house! Anansi held Tiger by the reins and beat him with his stick, crying, "Giddy-up, old horsey!" Miss Selina laughed until her sides hurt!

With a yowl of shame, Tiger threw the spider-man off his back and raced home.

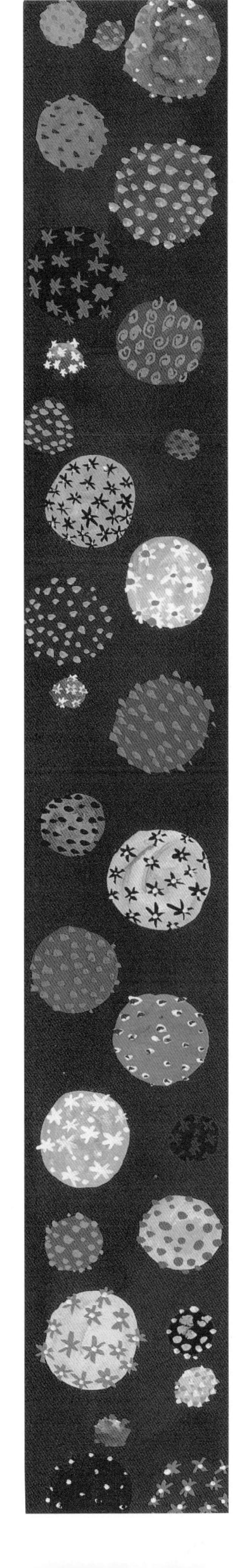

"I'll play a trick of my own on that trickster!" he growled.

Tiger lay on his bed and stuck his legs in the air, all stiff and still. It was very hard not to twitch a whisker or flick his tail, but Tiger didn't move a muscle. He wanted everyone to think he was dead. Anansi would creep up close to make sure—and then Tiger would pounce.

Tiger waited and waited and waited . . . and at last there was a knock at his door.

"Hello, Tiger!" a croaky voice shouted. "It's me, Turtle!"

Tiger kept as still and silent as a stone.

"No answer," sighed Turtle, "but I'd better make sure that Tiger's not at home." Turtle peeked through Tiger's window. "Help! Help!" he cried. "Tiger is dead!"

The news traveled like lightning through the forest and all the animals came running. Even Anansi joined the weeping, wailing crowd in Tiger's yard.

How odd that Tiger is suddenly dead! Anansi thought to himself. He turned to Duck and asked, "Did you hear that Tiger was sick?"

"No," sobbed Duck. "It happened very suddenly."

Anansi asked, "Was anyone with Tiger when he died?"

"No, he was all alone," sniffled Rat, shaking his head.

Anansi raised his voice and said, "Has anyone heard Tiger laugh?"

"Why no, Mr. Anansi!" everyone chorused, startled.

"Don't you know that dead creatures always have a last laugh?" Anansi said. "Perhaps Tiger isn't really dead."

Inside the house, Tiger heard every word.

How stupid of me not to know that! Tiger thought to himself. *I'd better prove I'm dead right away!*

Tiger threw back his head and roared with laughter.

"Aha!" cried Anansi. "Does *that* sound like a dead Tiger?"

The animals all looked at each other. How foolish they felt—but not half as foolish as Tiger!

By the time Tiger jumped out of bed, Anansi was long gone. So it was Anansi who had the last laugh, after all!

The Pot of Common Sense

Tonight, Grandma is sitting on the porch next to Grandpa, shelling peas into a large pot. The pot reminds Grandpa of another story....

Once upon a time, Anansi the spider-man collected all the common sense in the world and put it into a large pot. He wanted to keep it all for himself.

"How powerful and rich I am going to be!" Anansi chuckled, rubbing his hands with glee. "Everyone will have to come to me for advice, and I will only solve their problems if they pay me handsomely! But first, I must hide my common sense where no one will ever find it."

Anansi went up mountains, into caves, and behind waterfalls, looking for the perfect hiding place. Finally, he decided to keep the pot at the top of a very tall tree.

Anansi took some rope and tied one end to the pot and the other end around his neck. The pot hung down heavily in front of him, resting on his stomach. He stood in front of the tree. It was so tall he couldn't see the top.

"Here goes," sighed Anansi, and he began to scramble up the trunk, the heavy pot thumping against his stomach.

Now Anansi was a good climber, but this was much harder than usual. The pot got in the way, so Anansi's fingers couldn't get a good grip. Every time he hitched himself higher with his legs, the heavy pot swung to and fro and dragged him down. And the rope cut into his neck the whole time.

As he struggled and cursed, he heard ripples of laughter coming from the forest floor. Anansi squinted down and saw a little boy grinning up at him.

"You foolish spider-man!" the boy giggled. "Why don't you make things easier by hanging the pot *behind* you?"

Anansi couldn't believe his ears. He thought he had collected all the common sense in the world, and here was a little boy with a big piece of it! In a fury, Anansi grabbed the pot and hurled it as hard as he could. The little boy ran away, chuckling, and the pot smashed into a hundred pieces on the ground.

By the time Anansi had clambered down, the wind had blown the common sense away. It was scattered by the breeze all over the world. So, because of Anansi's selfishness, all creatures got a little bit of it!

THE BIG FLOOD

Grandpa says, "In the days when the world was young—"

"Stop!" the children shout. "Is this an Anansi story?"

"No," says Grandpa, looking puzzled.

"Then you have forgotten something very important," the boys and girls cry.

"Ah!" smiles Grandpa, nodding his head. "Crick crack!"

"Break my back!" reply the children.

And so Grandpa's story begins....

In the days when the world was young, a man chopped down a huge tree. He cut shoots from it and planted them in the ground so more trees would grow. Next he chopped part of the tree into logs and built himself a house. He rubbed other bits together and sparked up a fire. Finally he roasted some of the tree's nuts over the flames and ate them for his supper.

I should share this useful tree with my friends, thought the man. He gave shoots to the animals and birds so that they could grow trees of their own.

That was how it was in those days—Man helped the creatures, and the creatures helped Man. When boulders rolled down the mountainside onto Man's home, Gorilla moved them. When leaves grew over the paths, Dog guided Man by sniffing out a route. When Man was short of food, Ant scurried to and fro building grains of wheat into a pile for him to eat. Toucan flew over the treetops and shouted down to Man all the news of the forest.

One day, Man was enjoying a walk in the sunshine when he felt the ground squelching underneath his feet. He looked down and saw that water was running over the earth, washing away the grass and plants and turning the soil to mud. Man was worried and looked around to see where the water was coming from.

He was very surprised to find that the stream was gushing from the spot where he had cut down the huge tree. It spurted out of the ground in a wild fountain, bubbling and boiling. Man decided he'd better do something to stop it. Skillfully, he wove some reeds and leaves into an enormous, heavy, round basket. Then he dropped the basket over the frothing spring like a large lid. He stood back, satisfied. The thick basket muffled the roar of the water, and only a tiny trickle leaked out at the bottom. Man went on his way, whistling happily.

Soon afterward, Monkey came swinging through the trees. He noticed the strange, upturned basket and jumped down to examine it.

That looks like something Man has made, thought Monkey, grinning to himself. *I bet he's keeping some fruit underneath*. He decided to take a look.

Monkey grasped the basket and, with a big effort, lifted it off the ground. WHOOSH! A jet of water lifted Monkey into the air, then swept him off through the forest.

"Help!" cried Monkey, as he swirled along on the tide.

Man heard Monkey's terrified cries and realized that everyone was in great danger.

"Quick!" he yelled, "Run to the top of the highest mountain, then climb the tallest coconut trees!" As all the creatures raced for their lives, the skies darkened. Angry thunderclouds boomed overhead, lightning stabbed through the skies, and rain began to pour down. The storm turned the gushing spring into a rushing river that joined up with lakes and waterfalls. The water swamped the fields. It rose over the bushes and trees —and still it kept rising. Man and all the creatures clung to the treetops on top of the highest mountain. They watched as the last hill disappeared into the sea. Then all the world was water.

The rain didn't stop falling for five days, and even when it did, Man and the creatures couldn't see anything. Thick clouds hid the world from view. Man dropped a coconut into the darkness, and the animals heard it splash into the water a second later. Everyone shivered with terror. It wasn't safe to go down.

Every day for two weeks, Man dropped a coconut, and each time it was a little longer until the animals heard the splash. At last, they heard a loud WHOMP! as the coconut thudded onto dry land. All the creatures climbed gladly out of the trees. They were starving and raced away in all directions to find food. To their dismay, they saw that the flood had ruined the land. Fruit was soggy and rotten. Nuts and roots were damp and moldy. Crops were drowned. There was hardly anything left to eat.

The animals grew desperate—so desperate that some of them began to eat each other. Crocodile stole Turtle's eggs. Heron snatched Fish out of the river. Panther pounced on Rabbit. But Man was hungriest of all. He made a bow and arrows to shoot everything that flew. He carved a wooden spear to hunt everything that ran. He weaved a net and fishing line to catch everything that swam. He made traps with jagged teeth to snare everything that hopped or crawled.

All the creatures grew afraid of Man. They kept away from him and warned each other when he was coming. Everyone stopped talking to Man, and eventually he forgot how to speak their language. Only faithful Dog decided to stay with Man, and today Man is still able to understand him a little.

An owl suddenly hoots somewhere in the dark night, making the children jump. They wonder what Owl is saying and if he has been listening to the story....

"Wire bend," says Grandpa softly, and the girls and boys all sigh, "Story end."

The Water-Mama

There is a full moon tonight. It hangs huge and pale and round above the coconut palms, making the mountains look small.

"Tell us a scary story, Grandpa!" one little girl says.

Grandpa smiles and asks the children, "How scary?"

"VERY scary!" they shout with delight. Grandpa chuckles.

"All right," he says, and the children settle down and hold hands. "You have all heard of the strange things that come out at night in these islands, haven't you?" he asks.

The children silently nod their heads, and their eyes open wide.

"You have heard about the devil woman, who has one human foot and one cloven hoof, which she tries to hide with her long dress. And the half-dead zombies, who wander around haunting the living. And you must also have heard about the old women who shed their skins at night and turn into balls of flame. They fly into houses and suck the sweet blood of boys and girls!"

"Uggh!" giggle the children, huddling closer together.

"But perhaps you have not heard of the water-mama," says Grandpa, and the children shake their heads. "Crick crack!" he says in a spooky voice.

"Break my back!" the children whisper in reply.

And so Grandpa begins his story....

Down by the river is a patch of ground where nothing ever grows. A large, flat rock used to stand on this spot, but it tumbled into the water long ago. People say that on full-moon nights like tonight, the rock glowed and a woman appeared out of nowhere.

The woman had long, black, shiny hair down to her waist, and instead of legs she had a rainbow-silver fishtail. She sat on the rock in the moonlight, gazing at her reflection in the water and combing her hair with a golden comb. All the while, she sang softly to herself. People said that her voice was so lovely and her song was so sad that if you heard it, it would haunt your dreams forever. No one who caught sight of the woman ever saw her face. The moment anyone began to move toward her, she would dive into the water and disappear.

People said that if you got hold of the water-mama's comb, or a lock of her hair, she would grant you a wish.

So every full moon, men and women would come from far and wide to hide in the bushes by the river and wait for the water-mama. Sometimes she appeared and sometimes she didn't. But no one ever saw her face or held her comb or touched her hair—except for Ralph.

Ralph was a big, strong man who thought that talk of water-mamas and other spirits was just nonsense. He worked hard in the fields all day, and every evening he walked back along the river. In all the times he had passed by, Ralph had never once seen the water-mama.

One full-moon night, Ralph came home later than usual and there she was. She sat on her rock, combing her hair and singing her lovely, sad song. Ralph was enchanted and crept forward. He had heard all the stories, so he expected the water-mama to slip into the water and vanish. But suddenly she turned and looked straight at him. Her face was the most beautiful thing Ralph had ever seen. He gasped in amazement, and the water-mama smiled a sad smile. Then without a word, she plunged off the rock and was gone.

Ralph blinked and pinched himself. *I'm seeing things!* he thought. *I must have been working too hard!*

He hurried home to bed. But as he closed his eyes, the water-mama's song started to ripple through his head.

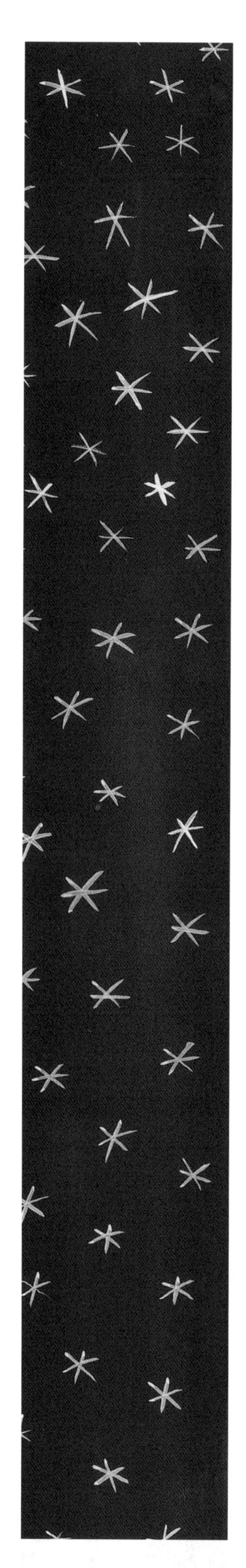

In his dreams, Ralph saw the water-mama again —and this time she spoke to him.

"Take this to remember me by," the water-mama said in a musical voice. She gave Ralph her golden comb. Twisted into it were a few strands of her long, black, shiny hair. "Now I will grant you one wish," she murmured.

Ralph couldn't believe his luck! He thought hard. What did he want most of all in the world?

"I want to be rich!" he cried with glee.

The water-mama smiled her sad smile.

"Very well," she sighed. "But keep the money a secret. If you don't, you will lose everything."

When Ralph woke up, he held a golden comb in his hand. In the center of the room there was a huge sack. Ralph rushed over and ripped it open. He couldn't believe his eyes. It was stuffed with money.

Ralph immediately forgot all about the water-mama's warning and rushed out to tell his family and friends. At first they thought that Ralph had gone mad, but he insisted that they should see it for themselves, and so they followed him back home.

The moment everyone laid their eyes on Ralph's amazing fortune, they went wild with greed. They turned on Ralph, punching and kicking him to the floor.

They filled their pockets and bags with the money and ran away with it, leaving Ralph for dead.

The boys and girls look up at Grandpa anxiously.

"What happened to him?" they cry.

"No one really knows," Grandpa says mysteriously. "But if one full-moon night you go down to the river, you will see the water-mama with a big, strong man standing beside her."

Everyone feels a shiver run down their spine.

"Now, wire bend," says Grandpa.

And the children reply, "Story end."

Index